Go Get Them

Are you a cheerleader or are you out in the field?

Go Get Them

Are you a cheerleader or are you out in the field?

Robert J. Shackleford

ASA PUBLISHING CORPORATION

AN INNOVATIVE OUTSOURCE BOOK PUBLISHING HYBRID

ASA Publishing Corporation
1285 N. Telegraph Rd., #376, Monroe, Michigan 48162
An Accredited Publishing House with the BBB
www.asapublishingcorporation.com

All Rights Reserved. No part of this publication may be reproduced, stored in a retrieval system or transmitted in any form or by any means electronic, mechanical, photocopying, recording or otherwise, without the prior written permission of the publisher. Author/writer rights to "Freedom of Speech" protected by and with the "1st Amendment" of the Constitution of the United States of America. This is a work of non-fiction; Christian education. Any resemblance to actual events, locales, person living or deceased that is not related to the author's literacy is entirely coincidental.

With this title/copyright page, the reader is notified that the publisher does not assume, and expressly disclaims any obligation to obtain and/or include any other information other than that provided by the author except with permission. Any belief system, promotional motivations, including but not limited to the use of non-fictional/fictional characters and/or characteristics of this book, are within the boundaries of the author's own creativity in order to reflect the nature and concept of the book. Unless otherwise indicated, all scripture quotations are taken from the King James Version of the Bible.

Any and all vending sales and distribution not permitted without full book cover and this copyright page.

Copyrights©2021 Robert J. Shackleford, All Rights Reserved
Book Title: Go Get Them *Are you a cheerleader or are you out in the field?*
Date Published: 01.08.2021 / Edition 1 *Trade Paperback*
Book ID: ASAPCID2380804
ISBN: 978-1-946746-91-7
Library of Congress Cataloging-in-Publication Data

This book was published in the United States of America.
Great State of Michigan

Table of Contents

Go Get Them

Are you a cheerleader or are you out in the field?

Robert J. Shackleford

INTRODUCTION

I was called into the ministry at the age of 12 years old. Many pastors would call me over to their church to run youth revivals to excite the young people of that day to live for Christ. I was so excited about preaching for Christ as a young boy, that whoever was around me got excited about Christ. I remember one year preaching in a tent youth revival in the inner city of Detroit. There were many young people there sitting and waiting to hear this little boy who was so excited about preaching anytime and at anyplace. As I began to preach, there were many kids there who received Jesus as Savior and Lord. Some of those kids came from the streets and had never committed their lives to Jesus Christ.

I really enjoyed going from church to church preaching, and even singing for Jesus. But when I got a few years older, I got caught up in a world of sin and fell through the cracks. It almost cost me my life being out of fellowship with God. I believe the problem was I didn't become a disciple of Jesus Christ. I preached about Him but never became Him. Also, I didn't go beyond the four walls of the church to win souls to Christ, which is the main purpose of preaching Christ. I had the ability to preach and see multitudes come to know Jesus, but I did not know how to get the harvest. Just like many of us, we go to church and get our shout-on mainly on Sundays but never go beyond the goosebumps.

I preached for many years before I became a disciple of Jesus Christ. After learning how to do what Jesus did, I began to see a greater manifestation of God beyond the four walls of the church. I remember the summer of 1993; I was invited to be a part of a tent meeting in Philadelphia, Pennsylvania. During that week of going into the devil's camp, I saw many people from off the street get saved. Some were drug dealers, gang members, prostitutes, and kids that lived in the public housing project.

This book is going to take you into another realm of God's great commission. You will find yourself dealing with some spiritual issues in every chapter of this book. But at the same time, God is going to show you how to go out into the field and get the ripe harvest.

So don't let anybody stop you from reading this book, for it is God's divine will that you do so. If you find yourself getting hungry for souls to get saved, wanting to be a disciple of Christ, learning new strategies, wanting to go and witness in the prison, and want that spirit of religion broking off of you, then I have fulfill my purpose of writing this book.

CHAPTER 1

The Heat is On: Religion vs. Disciples

"A student is not above His teacher, but everyone who is fully trained will be like His teacher" Luke 6:40

There is a real battle between religion and disciples of Jesus Christ. In many cases, religion seems to win out over discipleship. Why? It's easier to be religious than being a disciple of Jesus Christ. It does not challenge you to go to the next level in God when you are religious. But it will make your flesh go to the next level of bondage. The sinful flesh is design to be bound by something, whether you like it or not.

What is Religion?

The Latin meaning for religion is "to bind, back to bondage, oppress." Jesus spoke of three major things that religion will do to a person:

- It will kill
- It will steal
- It will destroy

It cost nothing to be religious. Anybody can go through the motions of looking like you are in the will of God, but the real truth is that it keeps you locked up and bound. Religion is being caught up in things.

- Denomination

- Church board
- Worship order
- A certain look
- Position in the church

It is so easy to get caught up in stuff and forget the real walk of God in the life of the believer. Most of us will hide behind the things in our local church and lose touch with God. I am not saying that we should not serve in the local church, but you must understand that religion is at the door waiting to come in and contaminate your service. If you are bound and are trying to go out into the field, guess what? Who so ever you touch most of the time will be bound also. The harvest field is not for the religious. Nor is it for the one who is going through the motion. Jesus said, ". . . unless your righteousness surpasses that of the Pharisees and the teachers of the law, you will certainly not enter the kingdom of heaven." Matthew 5:20

It is time that we stop trying to be like so many people and be like Jesus. The only true thing in this life is to imitate Jesus. And that's the bottom line!

A Disciple Gets Results

A disciple of Jesus Christ is aggressive in doing the things that God commissioned him to do. There are no lazy disciples in God's kingdom. Hearing and doing goes hand in hand in the life of the disciple. For the Bible says, "But the man who looks intently into the perfect law that gives freedom, and continues to do this not forgetting what he has heard, but doing it he will be blessed in what he does" James 1:25.

A disciple makes more disciples of Jesus Christ. Notice that I said, "More disciples of Jesus Christ." Not a disciple of you or Pastor Drybone. Once again, I must say it again because many believers want to make disciples of them, and that is a sign of being religious.

Jesus said in the gospel of Matthew 28:19 ". . . go and make disciples of all nations." That was a command of Jesus and not a suggestion. We love to obey when we read in the word of God that tells us to give ten percent of our gross income, because we want the window of heaven to open up for us. But when it comes down to going out and making disciples of Jesus, we don't want to, or we don't know how. You see, we fail to realize that Jesus said he would be with us even to the end of the world, if we go out. "And teaching them to obey everything I have commanded you. And surely I am with you always, to the very end of the age" Matthew 28:20.

The only thing that can kill a disciple is religion. So stay away from being religious. "It is for freedom that Christ has set us free. Stand firm, then, and do not let yourselves be burdened again by a yoke of slavery" Galatians 5:1.

Slavery is the state of man in which he is prevented from freely possessing and enjoying his life, a state opposed to liberty. Jesus said that it cost everything to be a disciple of Him. "If anyone comes to me and does not hate his father and mother his wife and children his brothers and sisters-yes, even his own life he cannot be my disciple" Luke 14:26-35.

CHAPTER 2

Discipleship-What are you doing?

As long as it is day, we must do the work of Him who sent me. Night is coming, when no one can work." John 9:4

The local church is the only institution that can make people like Jesus Christ. Therefore, the church must have a systematic anointed teaching ministry that will make men like Jesus. This means we got a lot of praying and studying of God's word to do. If secular books, motivational help, and even education can't make you a disciple, then the only thing that can is God's call out ones. I believe the world is waiting for the church to take her rightful place here on God's green earth. That is why most people get involved in gangs, cults and other false religious beliefs. They are looking for a strong structure and well discipline family-oriented setting. The church is that strong structure and well discipline family-oriented setting. We have to step up to the discipleship plate and get visible out in the streets.

Statistics said if a Muslim go out and witness to another person who is known in the community to be a crack head, thief, and a wife-beater, give him three months and he will be a disciple and back out in the street telling others about his faith. Not only that, but he will be off crack for good and loving his wife with a business in the same community. There is another statistic that says when a new believer comes into the church, in three months' time he falls through the cracks and leave the church and back out there where he came from. In knowing these statistics, I get very angry and fed up with all of the games that go on in the four walls of the church. Jesus called us to make disciples of Him.

What is Discipleship?

Webster's dictionary says discipleship is training that makes one like his teacher. The Greek lexical aid-(matheteo)-to train as a follower. For the goal of discipleship is not simply the attaining of information, but the experience and enjoyment of fellowship. Fellowship is the key ingredient to discipleship. Without it, you can forget about trying to disciple anyone. We must use saved hospitality, generosity, compassion, and friendship to someone else, thus showing ourselves as a disciple of Jesus.

This was the way Jesus did it alone with his disciples during the first century. We must come out of our selfish ways and start sitting down with unbelievers and teach them about Jesus and bring them into the fellowship with God's people. Also, there are a lot of believers sitting in the pews who aren't disciples. They just come to church every Sunday because it is the right thing to do. They do not know the first thing about praying, reading, and studying the word of God, or even how to live a saved sanctified life. They are just going through the motions of having church and not having a relationship with their Savior and Lord Jesus Christ. In the next chapter, I will talk more about fellowship and the importance of it.

Who ordered us to disciple people?

From the mouth of our Lord and Savior Jesus Christ, he has ordered us to make disciples. This was not a command of Moses, David, or even Paul, but of Jesus Christ. "Therefore go and make disciples of all nations, baptizing them in the name of the Father and of the Son and of the Holy Spirit" (Matthew 28:19). I can hear the heartbeat of Christ every time I read this verse. Jesus Christ being our Commander and Chief, has all rights to tell us what to do. He led the way for us to be disciple-makers, and he was the greatest example of teaching people the way of righteousness.

The presence of the Lord is always with us when we go out and make disciples of Jesus Christ (Matthew 28: 20). One of the greatest promises throughout the scriptures that we fail to remember is that he will be with us when we obey this powerful command, "and teaching them to obey everything I have command you. And surely I am with you always, to the very end of the age" Matthew 28:20. It may not put goosebumps on your body or make you fall out on the floor, but I can guarantee that God's presence will be with you. What more do you want from God other than his presence? If you want His presence in your life, then you know what you must do. Make disciples.

How can a believer disciple someone?

This is a good question that must be answered very carefully. Because I do not want to sound like I have the perfect answer. But God has truly anointed me in the area of church growth and evangelism. As a pastor who started with seven members in a Wendy's restaurant, and one month later, it grew to twenty-five members. I taught the members of my church to have a good relationship with Christ Jesus. Also, not to miss any worship services, if not possible. Then they were to go out and share what they had learned with someone else. That is how you can disciple someone all in one nutshell. Now let us discuss this in detail.

Relationship with Christ Jesus

In order for you to disciple someone else, you must have a relationship with Jesus. What I mean by this is we must know what he like, dislike, what makes him happy, know his commandment, know what pleases him, and know the great commission, frontwards and backwards. God desires that we love him with all of our heart, mind, soul, and strength and even with our bodies.

Having a good relationship with Christ is more than coming to church with a Bible under your arms. It's more than singing in the choir and going from conference to conference with all the series of the conference. It has to be more than getting in a prophecy line. How are you going to disciple someone, and you yourself don't know Christ in the fullest? The bad thing about this is that you will only make that person like you and not like Christ. Jesus said in John 15:7, "If you remain in me and my words remain in you, ask whatever you wish, and it will be given you." This whole verse is all about having a relationship with Christ. Why ask Christ for the harvest, and you do not have a relationship with him? Remember, to have a relationship with Christ is to know, obey, and to please him.

Do not miss Worship Service/Bible Study

There is much power when the saints come together on a weekly basis to celebrate and worship Christ Jesus. Many of us want to see people come to know Christ but fail to realize that worship service plays an important part. Something real special happens when the saints come together and show their love and respect for our soon coming King and for one another. Healing, impartation, deliverance, edification, and restoration take place in corporate worship.

We are not supposed to forsake the assembling together. Why would you lead someone to Jesus, and then you do not even worship with the rest of the disciples in your own local church?

Corporate Bible study has been neglected for many years in the body of Christ. We do not have a problem getting the religious out on Sunday mornings, but when it comes down to going to Bible Study, then we have a major problem. Bible study has been designed to instruct you to be a disciple and make disciples of Christ. If you do not come to Bible study on a regular basis, then it is a fact that you will not become a great disciple-maker. I know this is a strong statement, but you have to stop making excuses for missing Bible study.

Jesus said, “A student is not above his teacher, but everyone who is fully trained will be like his teacher” Luke 6:40. Fully trained in the Greek text means to instruct fully or completely, to equip and prepare intensively. The studying of God’s word is like a vacuum cleaner being used on a dusty carpet. Our life gets full of so much mess that we become what our mess is . . . like a dirty carpet. God cannot pour into us until we empty ourselves out of all the mess in us. This is why we must study God’s word on a daily basis in order to receive a fresh outpouring of God.

Our sinful flesh has an appetite that wants to eat and be satisfied every day. And at the same time, our spirit within our body has an appetite that must be fed every single day, or else it will die of spiritual malnutrition. Once you stop reading and studying God’s word, it will hinder you from growing up in the things of God. Also, sin finds its way into your life and began to start the process of destruction. Corporate worship and Bible study in the local church, when attended on a regular basis, will qualify you as a student that want to see others as students of Christ. You see, salvation is one beggar telling another beggar where he found bread. Disciples are beggars in Christ that always eat from Christ because he is really the bread of life.

How can the local church disciple the people being saved?

- Have a set time each week for the entire church to be taught.
- Identify teachers to make disciples.
- Come up with a strong curriculum for the saints

The reason believers fall through the crack is because they are not being made a disciple. Many become Muslims, Jehovah Witnesses, New Age, Christian Science and Mormon. Every cult or religion disciple his or her people with the intention of making him or her like his or her leader. They are disciplined spiritually and naturally, because of the teaching that they get every day.

The world desires to be a part of something that is tight. What I mean is that, they are used to order, structure, and things that are excellent. When we look at corporate America, there is a tight system in regarding training and leadership. The world will do whatever it takes to make it better in strengthening their business. They will send a new employee who has joined the company, to another state with everything paid for in full to learn the business. The bottom line in this example is they will disciple the newcomer to become like policy.

It is time that the church began to take the world into another level. They are waiting and watching. If you don't believe me, just listen to your unsaved friends, co-workers, neighbors, or people in the shopping mall. When you mess up, they are more at you for falling then you are. They have hope too and want to change their life around but need someone to show them the way.

I am amazed at how the church want to have the book of Acts experience, but do not want to do what they did after what they have experienced. The New Testament church went out and made disciples of Jesus Christ every day. They took what the apostle taught them and went from house to house, making people like Jesus Christ. All we have to do is what they did, and everybody in the world would probably be a disciple. Not only will the pastors, leaders, and other leaders in the local church know how to proclaim the gospel and disciple souls for Christ. But the little grandmas, doorkeepers, and car lot watchers of the church will know how to do the same thing. The church can do it because God has designed his church to do so.

CHAPTER 3

Born To Do Evangelism

"For the son of man came to seek and to save what was lost."

Luke 19:10

Evangelism is the heartbeat of God. God's passion is that everybody has eternal life through his son Jesus Christ. "The Lord is not slow in keeping his promise, as some understand slowness. He is patient with you, not wanting anyone to parish, but everyone to come to repentance" 2 Peter 3:9. If that is God's passion, then once he has saved us, then He has put in us a special hunger and desire to see people saved also. "You did not choose me, but I chose you and appointed you to go and bear fruit-fruit that will last . . . " John 15:16. Jesus was on earth walking around doing the Father's business. His hold aim was to save that which was lost. Therefore, our hold aim is that we bear fruit and fruit that shall last. "This is to my Father's glory, that you bear much fruit, showing yourselves to be my disciples" John 15:8. Human lives are the only thing that will last. I do not care what you buy in life: cars, houses, buildings, etc. It will not last like souls.

WHAT IS EVANGELISM? G.G.B.

Going to the lost, giving them the gospel where they are, and bring them into the fellowship with God's people. "Ask the Lord of the harvest, therefore, to send out workers into his harvest field" Matthew 9:38. "Go rather to the lost sheep of Israel. As you go, preach this message: The kingdom of heaven is near" Matthew 10: 6,7. "But Barnabas took him and brought him to the apostles. He told them how Saul on his journey had seen the Lord and that the Lord had spoken to him, and how in Damascus he had preached fearlessly in the name of Jesus. So Saul stayed with them and moved about freely in Jerusalem, speaking boldly in the name of the Lord" Acts 9: 27,28.

The Problem

There is a major problem among the believers. Statistics say only four out of one hundred believers know how to evangelize. Our country, city, and neighborhoods are dying because of the believer's lack of knowledge.

The Solution

The solution to this problem is that we must understand four things:

Evangelism is an individual activity. Before there was an Acts Chapter 2 event, Jesus said, ". . . and you will be my witness in Jerusalem, and in all Judea and Samaria, and to the ends of the earth" Acts 1:8. This was a personal command from Jesus Christ, our Savior and Lord to all individuals. You personally must get excited about G.G.B. and find ways to be an effective soul winner. Do not wait on somebody to witness in your community. You do it (Nike).

The entire local church must do evangelism "So the Word of God spread. The number of disciples in Jerusalem increased rapidly, and large number of priests became obedient to the faith," Acts 6:7. The church in Jerusalem grew because they corporately did evangelism. They didn't have a department in the church that did it all. "Then Jesus came to them and said, all authority in heaven and on earth has been given to me. Therefore go and make disciples of all nations, baptizing them in the name of the Father and of the Son and of the Holy Spirit, and teaching them to obey everything I have commanded you. And surely I am with you always, to the very end of the age" Matthew 28:18-20. It isn't a one-time thing; it's a lifestyle.

Explanation

Go – is motion one place to another. It has nothing to do with the inside of a church building. It has nothing to do with prophesying to someone in the church's parking lot or restroom. It doesn't have anything to do with singing in the choir on Sunday mornings. Jesus said go, and he meant right now. By the way, this was not a suggestion but a command.

Make – make disciples of Jesus Christ. It did not say make Christians, but disciples. That means we must sit at Jesus' feet to learn and imitate him and then train others to be like him (Luke 6:40). We do not mind paying our tithes, praying at six in the morning, or even fasting every now and then. But when it comes down to "make," we get lazy, afraid, and forgetful. The word "make" does not mean that we must force people to be like Jesus. But it denotes making a special effort to train and teach people the things of Christ.

Nation – it means ethnic groups, which consist of a multitude of people. Jesus intended that his bride go out beyond their little neighborhood, community, city, state, and country to do evangelism. Evangelism breaks down racism in the life of many people. It is a universal thing that God had ordained. That's why we need power to do this. Because going to nations is going into the devil's camp and taking back what he has stolen.

Satan desire that nations be divided, confuse, and out there by themselves. But God's aim is that the church go to all nations and give them the gospel so that they may have peace with God and have the peace of God.

The gospel is twofold: Spiritual and Natural

Spiritual

Jesus said . . . no one could enter the kingdom of God unless he is born of water and the spirit, John 3:5. The new life starts in the inward man. The sinner becomes a new creation through Christ Jesus "Therefore, if anyone is in Christ, he is a new creation: the old has gone, the new has come." 2 Corinthians 5:17. His life is completely changed by faith with no help from the flesh and no works that one may want to do. It makes no difference what condition the unsaved may be in when he comes to Jesus. The old man is totally gone forever and ever.

One thing about the spiritual aspect of the gospel is that God will use people to snatch the unsaved out of the pathway of hell. That is why we must make ourselves available for God to use us at any time and at any place. We should never get so comfortable in life that we don't share the gospel on a regular basis. It should be a joy to go out and see lives change and watch the devil get mad and sit his self-down somewhere.

Natural

This is one subject that the church has dropped the ball. Jesus Christ demonstrated the gospel in the natural: he provided food, healed the sick, cast out demons, comforted the comfortless, accepted children, and was a friend to the unsaved. Jesus reached out his hand and touched the man. "I am willing, he said. Be clean! And immediately the leprosy left him, Luke 5:13. When Jesus came into Peter's house, he saw Peter's mother-in-law lying in bed with a fever. He touched her hand and the fever left her, and she got up and began to wait on him. When evening came, many who were demon-possess were brought to him, and he drove out the spirits with a word and healed all the sick Matthew 8:14-16. At that time the disciples came to Jesus and asked, who is the greatest in the kingdom of heaven? He called a little child and had him stand among them. And he said: I tell you the truth, unless you change and become like little children, you will never enter the kingdom of heaven, Matthew 18:1-3. Jesus was the greatest example in touching people in a natural way, because of his compassion for souls.

We must learn from the master (Jesus), how to use whatever we get our hands on to bring the unsaved to Christ. Jesus saw two fishes, he used it to bring glory to God. He saw a pool of water, and he used it to heal a blind man. My point here is that Jesus used the natural to help lives. We should use whatever we can to bring glory to God. We must not preach a one-sided gospel. The church is the healing hand of Jesus Christ. God uses the church to touch lives in the natural. So let us preach the gospel that Jesus preached. The Spirit of the Lord is on me, because he has anointed me to preach good news to the poor. He has sent me to prisoners and recovery of sight for the blind, to release the oppressed, to proclaim the year of the Lord's favor, Luke 4:18-19.

Many of us are very selfish and stingy. We don't want to give to people's needs unless we have some motives behind it. We don't mind giving to our friends or a family member. But God requires us to go deeper than that. If you love those who love you, what reward will you get? Are not even the tax collectors doing that? And if you greet only your brothers, what are you doing more than others? Do not even pagans do that? Matthew 5:46, 47. It is all about the gospel being preached with a heart to see people saved. This is the hour to go to the next level of reaching out to people with compassion dripping from our hearts.

There must be a balance in our presenting the gospel of Jesus Christ. You may love to go out and give a testimony about your life and how Christ saved you. However, if you don't touch people in a natural way, something may go wrong even in your personal ministry. What I mean is, you may be planting a seed of self-edification? Also, the spirit of religion may come in and take over. You must remember salvation is a two-fold process: spiritual and natural.

Jesus just didn't feed people to make a name for himself. He didn't heal people just to draw a crowd to show

how powerful He was. But he did all of these miracles to reveal the gospel in action. In the same way we must reveal the gospel in action that many may see Jesus in a greater way. No matter what it takes, please touch somebody with the touch of love, power, compassion, and strength.

CHAPTER 4

Mastering Your Community

"The fruit of the righteous is a tree of life, and He who wins souls is wise." Proverbs 11:30

Every local church should be so happy that God has placed her in a community. A community is a group of people who live in the same area, and a group of people who have the same interests, religion, race, etc. The community is an unseen Jewel for the church and needs to be tapped into. Everything a church needs whether it be spiritual or natural, it is in the community. I do not know why the church is so afraid to go out and get the gold, which will enrich the entire ministry of the church. Community is very much key in having a successful and soul-winning church. I want to share with you what it means to master your community. Many of us are looking outside of our community, trying to get community church growth. Some are not looking at all; therefore, they will never get the God kind of results.

The Bible said in Acts 1:8, But you will receive power when the Holy Spirit comes on your, and you will be my witnesses in Jerusalem and in all Judea and Samaria and to the ends of the earth. Saints, we have to stop overlooking our Jerusalem (church community). I see great principles about mastering your community in Acts 1:8. Jesus said, "you will be my witnesses in Jerusalem." He did not say you shall be my witnesses in Egypt, Rome, or Galilee first. He said Jerusalem.

Every local church has a Jerusalem, their community. In our community we see great opportunities in demonstrating the power of the Holy Spirit.

In the community of Jerusalem Jesus went up, the Holy Spirit came down, and the people went out. Through the message of Peter, three thousand souls were baptized and were added to the newborn church in one day. A day or two later, Peter and John were teaching the people and proclaiming in Jesus the resurrection of the dead. And, the number of men grew to about five thousand. The early church truly mastered their community through the power of the Holy Spirit. The saints had all things in common in terms of natural things. The saints went from house to house, fellowshipping with each other in the community. People saw the real deal about the power and love of Jesus.

People in the community, needs were met through the church. If you needed a healing, the church was used by God to meet that need. If the dead needed to be raised, the church met that need. If the community needed some kind of spiritual control and monitor, the church set up small groups in the community. Rapid church growth took place in the community.

"So the word of God spread. Because of the gospel, many of those who lied and disliked Jesus in the community became obedient to the faith. The number of disciples in Jerusalem increased rapidly, and a large number of priests became obedient to the faith Acts 6:7.

In the community of my church, we had one of the meanest motorcycle gangs of the city. Also, there were thugs and serious drug dealers in the neighborhood. However, that did not stop our entire church in exhibiting the power of the Holy Spirit in the community. I remember we had the streets blocked out so we can give back to the community. We gave away food, clothes, preached the gospel, and much more kingdom things. During the outreach event, one of the key drug dealers came up to me and asked if I was the pastor. I told him yes I am, and how may I help you. He said that your church is during a great job in the community. Also, he asks if he can leave his son at the event and if I have any trouble with anybody, let him know.

I remember our entire church went out to share the love and power of Jesus Christ in the community. We did this week after week until one day a gang member of the bike club came to me and offered his help. He wanted to keep the grass cut on the church property. He was touch by what the church was doing in the community. He saw people that grew up with him walking to church. He saw people that grew up with him giving their life to Christ and living a changed life in the community. I believe we left a great impact on his life. He saw the real deal of genuine love, and wanted to show how grateful he and the bike gang were.

In most communities there are schools, churches, banks, playgrounds, and grocery stores, etc. And at these various places, there are great opportunities to share the gospel of Jesus Christ. We need to stop praying that God would bring sinners into our churches. Jesus would want us to go get them and give them the good news where they are and bring them to church. We have a great harvest at the schools, parks, banks, grocery stores. Our next leaders are in our community, and waiting for someone to tell them about Jesus. Therefore, we need to master our community by looking deep into what is in the community to see how we can serve, love, and share what God has given us for them.

I called the principle of a public school in our

community to ask if I may speak to the students about overcoming failure and fear. The answer I got from the principle was stunning. "Pastor Shackleford, please come and do whatever you do, we need help," she said. This is what I needed to hear in order for me to move forward in winning the kids to Christ. It was on a Friday morning that I brought with me the praise team, step dance team, and the hip-hop team. I want you to know that there was such a demonstration of the power of God.

The principle had all the doors locked so that no one could leave or enter. All the students and all of the teachers were required to attend the service. The harvest was so ripe and ready for God's kingdom. The place was so packed with souls from wall to wall ready for harvest. Excitement was in the air throughout the whole time that we were there. Would you believe that after I preached Jesus, I had an altar call? Yes, right in the community where my church was located, I preached Jesus in a public school, and over 300 souls came to Jesus Christ. What a sight to see, young people were clapping their hands, they were rejoicing, weeping, and sharing their hurt.

Saints, we do not need to look very far in searching for

a great harvest. You need to know that your blessing is right in your back yard. Get up and go get the harvest in your community, where you will reap what you sow. Believe it or not, you have preachers, musicians, ushers, singers, and community leaders right in your backyard. In your backyard there are schools, playgrounds, stores, block clubs, recreation centers, and people of all ages. Mastering your community is being consistent in sharing the gospel to the ready harvest that is in your community.

Most urban communities have public transportation where you can get around town easily. There is great opportunity in sharing Jesus at the bus stop. People who are waiting for their bus to come cannot go anywhere but wait for it. I have experienced the power of God many times at a bus stop. I stand at the bus stop like I want to catch a bus. However, I do not catch a bus because I want to catch souls. A few Saturdays ago, my church went out to do bus stop ministry. Tony was frustrated because his bus took too long in coming. I walked up to Tony and began to share the gospel with him. Just to show you how awesome our God is and how ripe the harvest, Tony gave his life to Christ.

There was a social service office in our community, and the social workers would take their lunch at 12:00 noon. It left the clients who needed assistance in public help sitting waiting for their worker to return. Some of the clients left for lunch and some stay in their seats. However, I took advantage of the moment (harvest moment).

I would go out Monday through Friday sharing the gospel of Jesus Christ during the lunch period. I walk the streets praying for people and demonstrating the power of God for about one hour a day. Many of those clients received Jesus as Lord and Savior, and some would receive healing physically and emotionally. Everyone that I ask to pray for did not refuse the prayer but received it gladly. You see saints, there is a great harvest right in your community. Be consistent in working your own Jerusalem.

In your community, there should be trees of life and there should be saints who are full of God's wisdom. The Bible said, "The fruit of the righteous is a tree of life, and he who wins souls is wise" Proverbs 11:30. The righteous, by the performance of his duty to his neighbors, bring, as it were, life and healing to them, and "the wise man wins souls," attracts them to himself, and induces them to follow his example. The one who win souls in the community is as fowler doth birds, or a fisherman fishes; that makes it his design and business, and uses all his skill and diligence to gain souls to God, and to pluck them out of the snare of the devil; is wise.

Saints, we are the tree of life, the branch of the living vine. It is worth saying it again; we are the tree of life, and their influence upon earth, like the fruits of that tree, supports and nourishes the spiritual life in many. The wise believer will never let souls that are in their community stay in the camp of the enemy. The wise will always pray for their community. The wise will always have a good plan in winning souls to Christ. The wise will never let laziness and fear win the battle in their life. I need you to remember that your community is your community. So get up and do not let nobody win your stuff, which belongs to you.

CHAPTER 5

Children's Ministry

. . . Let the little children come to me, and do not hinder them, for the kingdom of heaven belongs to such as these"
Matthew 19:14

As you know, we are losing our kids every day. In today's society our children are faced with drugs, troubled homes, alcoholism, poverty, molestation, rape, violence, and the new aged movement. In the children's ministry, the church's goal is to reach these kids and make them strong and stable kids for Jesus Christ.

We cannot be too holy that we forget our children who sit with us in the church on Sunday mornings. Many of them come to church with their parents having many issues that we as adults don't have a clue what's going on. And then before you know it, our kids are young adults with those same issues cover up with a flavor of religion. Once they become adults, then the cycle starts all over again with a new set of family. We cannot forget them any longer, for they have souls too. The church must have a special program designed specifically for them. The focus of these programs is to make our children disciples of Jesus at an early age.

This can happen by the teaching from God's word on a level of their understanding. Also, the parents have to demonstrate a Godly example in front of their children. "Nor should there be obscenity, foolish talk or coarse joking, which are out of place, but rather thanksgiving." Eph. 5:4

The children must be taught how to pray and live a consecrated life every day for their Lord and Savior Jesus Christ.

"Listen, my Son, to a father's instruction; pay attention and gain understanding. I give you sound learning, so do not forsake my teaching. When I was a boy in my father's house still tender, and an only child of my mother, he taught me and said, "Lay hold of my words with all your heart; keep my commands and you will live. Get wisdom, get understanding; do not forget my words or swerve from them."

Do not forsake wisdom, and she will protect you; love her, and she will watch over you. Wisdom is supreme; therefore get wisdom. Though it cost all you have, get understanding. Esteem her, and she will exalt you; embrace her, and she will honor you. She will set a garland of grace on your head and present you with a crown of splendor. Listen, my son, accept what I say, and the years of your life will be many. I guide you in the way of wisdom and lead you along straight paths. When you walk, your steps will not be hampered; when you run, you will not stumble. Hold on to instruction, do not let it go; guard it well, for it is your life. Do not set foot on the path of evil men. Avoid it, do not travel on it; turn from it and go on your way. For they cannot sleep till they do evil; they are robbed of slumber till they do evil; they are robbed of slumber till they make someone fall. They eat the bread of wickedness and drink the wine of violence.

The path of the righteous is like the first gleam of dawn, shining ever brighter till the full light of day. But the way of the wicked is like deep darkness; they do not know what makes them stumble. My son, pay attention to what I say; listen closely to my words. Do not let them out of your sight, keep them within your heart; for they are life to those who find them and health to a man's whole body. Above all else, guard your heart, for it is the wellspring of life. Put away perversity from your mouth; keep corrupt talk far from your lips. Let your eyes look straight ahead, fix your gaze directly before you. Make level paths for your feet and take only ways that are firm. Do not swerve to the right or the left. Keep your foot from evil." Proverbs 4

Parents, when you release your children to go to school every day, hoping that they will receive the best education from that institution, it is very important that you cover them in much prayer. They need to have clear instructions from the word of God. In this society, we are dealing with a spiritual madman monster out there. We cannot let our guards down by going through our religious motions. The devil doesn't mind you taking your children to church, as long as you don't train them in righteousness.

I went to a certain church one Sunday, and found myself getting very angry and ready to smack the preacher on the back of his head. I saw many of the kids that attended the morning worship sleeping, playing, and even walking around just to get away from the foreign country (the morning service). All of this was taking place while the pastor was preaching. That pastor was so excited about preaching and doing his Sunday morning duties that he forgot the lifeline of his church. Evangelism is more than seeing adults saved. It is reaching our young people with a desire to see them living a fulfilled life for Christ.

God called most strong leaders and prophets in the Bible at an early age. Let us look at King Joshia, the southern king of Israel. God called him at an early age of nine, to lead and reign over a nation. He was instructed to tear down the idols that were placed in the temple of God. The famous Moses, from a little baby boy, was destined to lead millions out of Egypt into the wilderness so they can worship God. The mother of Jesus was chosen not as a full-grown woman but as a little girl to give birth to the Savior of the world. What I am saying God is calling our children's generation too. Therefore, we must get busy in the field of young people and start saving them.

I believe children's ministry starts at home with mom and dad. Yes, your home is a sanctuary where your children can know God in a great way. Ministry at home with your kids is when they begin to respect and honor God. Your kids learn how to pray, read God's word, and witness to other kids when it is a home of ministry.

I remember when I was a kid growing up in my father's house, he would teach me scriptures to learn that I may share it with other kids. I would even learn new songs in our home to sing it to my friends. And now I have been a blessing to hundreds of thousands of people because of the ministry that I was brought up in at my home.

Why save our children?

This is the only way to preserve righteousness on earth. The devil wants to kill them at an early age. To keep the church on fire and alive, Jesus said don't forsake the children. "People were also bringing babies to Jesus to have him touch them. When the disciples saw this, they rebuked them. But Jesus called the children to him and said, "Let the children come to me, and do not hinder them. The kingdom of God belongs to such as these. I tell you the truth; anyone who will not receive the kingdom of God like a little child will never enter it." Luke 18:15-17

In order for us to have a land of righteousness, we must save our children. The children are our inheritance that will keep our nation set apart for God. We are now determining what our children will be in the future. If we are righteous practically, then our seed will be righteous. If we take a stand for holiness, then our children will become holy chasers. Where there is righteousness, then our children will embrace it.

Satan does not know your future, but he knows the pattern of a sold-out witness for Christ. That is why he tries to keep moms and dads at war against each other. Where there is trouble in the home, know for sure that it is the devil behind it. But when the sold-out mom and dad began to operate under the power of God in the home, then the children will be strong and mighty in God. I do not care what's going on in the school, community, and even over friend's house, your children will stand for holiness.

The Bridge

Our kids need a bridge to help them cross over to unconditional love, peace, deliverance, education, safety, and second chance. God has given our children a special bridge, and it is our youth pastors, ministries of education, teachers, and youth directors. Our youth pastor is just as important than the senior pastor in our local churches. For they are our special bridge that God has put in the lives of the youth. Senior pastors must release them to go forth in there calling, to reach and train the youth that they may be young disciples of Jesus Christ.

God's anointing is on this generation to reach the unreachable. Many of these kids have been walking the streets late at night telling other kids about Christ. There is a holy boldness in this new generation to go into those rough places that none of us would go into if you paid us one million dollars to do so.

CHAPTER 6

License to Kill: Marriage and Evangelism

Subdue

The command of God in marriage was to subdue. Yes, God has given us a license to conquer, overcome, and control the spiritual atmosphere right here on earth. We did not ask to subdue, so therefore, God has something in mind for us as married couples. What God has in mind is that we begin to use our spiritual license to move every hindrance that will stop us from seeing multitudes come to know Christ. Subdue will allow us to conquer the impossible that comes into our marriage life. Subdue will allow us to adventure out into the deep waters of opportunities. With subdue, we can do anything but fail.

Notice God did not say that we should subdue people but the earth. Many times we violate this command by trying to control our husband and wife. We find ourselves unhappy in our marriage because we misuse God's authority, which was meant for the purpose of divorce, controlling things and not our spouse. Therefore, marriage has enough power in itself to overcome poverty, sickness, fear, laziness, and unforgiveness. So we must get up and enjoy what God has given us in our marriage, for it is the ability to subdue the earth, and that's powerful.

Many times we as believers stop overcoming the things

that want to get us down. It is the devil's aim to break us down through life situations so that we let our guards down. The devil knows that marriage is divine and powerful, so therefore he attacks it until the marriage of the believer breaks down and end up in the courtroom. Once it gets into the courtroom, the believer takes his/her eyes off the true enemy (Satan) and start focusing in on each other. Then the enemy starts the generational cycle of poverty, sickness, fear, laziness, and unforgiveness.

It is our responsibility in our walk with God to maintain victory. Victory and subdue go hand and hand with an undertone of warfare. We must clearly understand that God's word sets the tone for us concerning our victory. The Bible teaches us from Genesis to Revelation that "God is a warrior, the battle is the Lord and not mine, to him who overcomes I will give the right to eat from the tree of life, which is in the paradise of God, to him who overcomes and does my will to the end, I will give authority over the nations, he will rule them with an iron scepter."

Abba Father gives us the victory and not our job, money, love ones, pastor or even the church. He gives it through the vehicle of Christ. "The sting of death is sin, and the power of sin is the law. But thanks be to God! He gives us the victory through our Lord Jesus Christ." 1 Corinthians 15:56,57

There is nothing that the devil can do about this, even if he tries. He cannot change the fact that God gives the victory to every believer for divine purposes. I like to give you the meaning of victory or subdue before I explain the three purposes of victory.

The Greek word is Nike-it means to triumph, conquer, and overpower. In one sense, it means attaining the mastery. There is a secular company that is spreading the good news that the church should be doing. Every time you see it on television or see your son/daughter wearing their product, they are telling us to "Nike" just do it, be an overcomer. Every year Nike spends millions of dollars on advertisement in order that we "Christians" get the message just do it and be victorious. We as disciples, should follow the heartbeat of God to do His will and not put the momentum behind this secular companies' advertisements. Now what doesn't hurt us must make us better.

With a license to kill from God, we already have the victory. It is what Jesus Christ has done on the cross for us. So do not listen to that liar, the devil, when it comes down to maintaining victory in your life. Married couples have all rights to go into the devil's camp and get our belongings. Soul winning is subduing, overcoming, and winning the victory.

Victory/Subdue Purpose

There are three major purposes for victory in the life of the believer over the sinful nature. "So I say, live by the Spirit, and you will not gratify the desires of the sinful nature. For the sinful nature desired what is contrary to the Spirit, and the Spirit what is contrary to the sinful nature. They are in conflict with each other, so that you do not do what you want. But if you are lead by the Spirit, you are not under law. The acts of the sinful are obvious, sexual immorality, impurity and debauchery, idolatry and witchcraft; hatred, discord, jealousy, fits of rage, dissension, selfish ambition, factions and envy; drunkenness, orgies, and the like. I warned you, as I did before, that those who live like this will not inherit the kingdom of God."

In these passages of scriptures, it's talking about war and conflict between the Spirit and the sinful nature.

God has given us weapons to hold our own ground of victory, and it is called the "Fruit of the Spirit." Fruit signifies that all nine are normal results of the life of the Holy Spirit. These qualities stand in sharp contrast to the disruptive "evil results" of a sinful nature (v.19). These spirits foster and build communities of evil spirit.

As I stated before, victory is ours already, but we must maintain it every day. God provides complete armor to protect us from all kinds of evil and temptation. The armor helps us to stand firm against all strategies and tricks of the devil.

The strategies are the result of superhuman craftiness, capable of drawing careless saints into sin. The believer's life is a struggle; it requires decision and effort. Our real enemy is not human flesh and blood, but the devil and his hosts. These evil rulers and authorities of the unseen world have so blinded the world to spiritual values that unregenerate people cannot understand God or His will. The forces of evil are superhuman, but they are not all-powerful. God has given us adequate power for to take back and maintain victory over them.

The Apostle Paul wrote to the church in Rome to let them know that God gave them the Spirit of God to deliver them from the power of the sinful nature. Now let us turn and read Romans 8:36, 37. Even the scriptures say, "For your sake we are killed every day; we are being slaughtered like sheep."

"No despite all these things, overwhelming victory is ours through Christ, who loved us." NLT

Let me ask you a question. Why do you think God gave us victory over sinful nature? There are two reasons why he did. First, sin separates us from God which ends in death. Secondly, it is like suffocating him. Therefore, God has given us tools to keep us on top of life situations. He desires that we have an eternal love life with him, and that we become a sweet smell in his nostrils.

"Who say, keep away; don't come near me, for I am too sacred for you! Such people are smoke in my nostrils, a fire that keeps burning all day." Isa.65:5

"For the wages of sin is death, but the gift of God is eternal life in Christ Jesus our Lord." Romans 6:23

Over The World

"For everyone born of God overcomes the world? This is the victory that has overcome the world, even our faith. Who is it that overcomes the world? Only he who believes that Jesus is the Son of God." John 5:4-5

When we are born of God through trusting in Jesus, God puts his own life in us. Thus, we are able to overcome the temptations, false teachings, and persecutions of the sinful world. The power of this ungodly world is totally against every believer. The word "world" in the Greek means kosmos: everything that belongs to the world that is hostile to God and ruled by the devil. "Now is the time for judgment on this world; now the prince of this world will be driven out." John 12:31

Now let us look at 1 John 2:15-17. "Do not love the world or anything in the world. If anyone loves the world, the love of the father is not in him. For everything in the world-the cravings of the sinful man, the lust of the eyes and the boasting of what he has and does-comes not from the father but from the world. The world and its desires pass away, but the man who does the will of God lives forever."

God is commanding us to stop loving the world, which mean, human life in opposition of God. If we live according to the world's values, we do not love God. That is why we must overcome the world and the spirit of this world.

Over Satan

"Submit yourselves, then, to God. Resist the devil and he will flee from you." Too many of us are literally afraid of the devil. It is because we know how to do everything accept maintaining victory in our life. Something is wrong with this picture. First of all God said humble yourself before him. Humble is the first step to victory in the life of every believer. If we humble ourselves you can be for sure that God will get the glory in every situation.

Satan is a liar and the truth is not in him. Why should we believe a liar? That is why we have power over him in this lifetime; where there is hate, bitterness, and anger. He heard God tell the first married couple to subdue the earth, be fruitful and prevail against. Therefore, he will try with all of his deceptive tricks to stop God's oo7's (married couples), from taking over his camp.

To Rule

To rule is to have dominion, prevail against, reign, and overtake. This is a special responsibility that God has given the couple. God said for us to rule over the fish of the sea; spiritually speaking, we have power to prevail whatever is under our feet. We are to rule over the birds of the air, which gives us power above our head. Livestock are rule by us. Which mean that we have power over the surface of the earth. Also, we have power and dominion over all the earth. There is no doubt that God has given us power over wherever we may go.

There is ruling power available for every married couple that loves the name of God. The Power, He has given us is to take control of oneself in every area of our life. We cannot let the devil any longer come into our camp and steal what God has given us.

In essence, the God kind of marriage should be fruitful. Meaning it should display Christ's character. "Wives submit to your husbands as to the Lord. For the husband is the head of the wife as Christ is the head of the church, the body, of which he is Savior. Now as the church submits to Christ, so also wives should submit to their husbands in everything. Husbands, love your wives just as Christ loves the church and gave himself up for her to make her holy, cleansing her by the washing with water through the word, and to present her to himself as a radiant church, without stain or wrinkle or any other blemish, but holy and blameless. In this same way, husbands ought to love their wives as their own bodies. He who loves his wife loves himself. After all, no one ever hates his own body, but he feeds and cares for it, just as Christ does the church-for we are members of his body. For this reason, a man will leave his father and mother and be united to his wife, and the two will become one flesh. This is a profound mystery-but I am talking about Christ and the church. However, each one of you also must love his wife as he loves himself, and the wife must respect her husband."

Marriage is to make more people like Christ. For God is into great numbers (multiplication) when it comes down to winning souls (the will of God), the husband and wife act as a couple equal in knowledge of God's word and the work of the church. "He began to speak boldly in the synagogue. When Priscilla and Aquila heard him, they invited him to their home and explained to him the way of God more adequately." Acts 18:26

"Greet Priscilla and Aquila, my fellow workers in Christ Jesus. They risked their lives for me. Not only I but all the churches of the Gentiles are grateful to them. Greet also the church that meets at their house . . ." Romans 16:3-5

We are to fill the earth with God-fearing people. "Therefore go and make disciple of all nations, baptizing them in the name of the Father, and of the Son and of the Holy Spirit." Matthew 28:19

"Has not the Lord made them one? Yes! And why one? Because he was seeking godly offspring. So guard yourself in your spirit, and do not break faith with the wife of your youth." Marriage is a license to kill Satan's deeds, which is our only enemy. Marriage is spiritual warfare against the kingdom of darkness. Therefore, God's divine purpose for husbands and wives is warfare.

Kicking the devil's natural butt

In the early stage of my marriage, my wife and I had some funny and interesting moments. Our first big fight was when we were preparing our church for our monthly church love feast. My wife was disturbed at me because I did not mop the church fellowship hall floor the way her grandmother did. We both yelled at each other from the top of our lungs, and when it was time for the saints to come for fellowship, we had to pretend that everything was all right. My point in telling you this story is that the devil doesn't mind you being religious and going through the motion in your marriage. Also, he loves for the married couple to war against each other over little stuff, so that bitterness, hatred, and unforgiveness can enter in.

If Satan can get the married couple off focus on the real purpose of marriage, then he has won the battle in the life of the married couple. For we are so quick to fall for the "I blame you" syndrome. We lose sight on why we are here together, with no idea that Satan is our real enemy.

I have counseled with more couples these days then I have ever done in the early years of ministry. I found out that the bottom line problem is that 99% of everyone that I've counseled was off focus and misled by the devil. If you are having problems in your marriage, go back and reestablish the commands of God in the book of Genesis 1:26-30. Beginning at the beginning, with an understanding of what godly marriage was meant to be and place it on your natural enemy, Satan.

When two people come together and enter into the marriage covenant, at that point they have license to kill the work of Satan, who is our real enemy. Godly marriage is spiritual warfare against the kingdom of darkness. Which means, there are things that happens in the spiritual realm every day to stop the godly marriage from winning souls for Christ. God intended that the Holy Spirit filled person come together with a great understanding of what the purpose of marriage is and to watch each other back in prayer and win souls to Christ.

God takes marriage very seriously and so does the

devil. God said be fruitful and multiply, Satan said to destroy the fruit or eat the fruit and you shall live (which is death in reality). God said to fill the earth with God-like people, and Satan said fill the earth with ungodly people.

This is what I am trying to say there is something in the spiritual realm that is truly happening. God is the originator of righteousness, and Satan is a "copycat." When he tries to duplicate God, it turns out perverted and evil. This is why God gave marriage couples license to kill what is not of God, and to go out into the devil's camp and take back what he has stolen.

Jesus Christ used marriage as an example of a relationship between him and the church. Christ is the husband, and the church is the wife. The wife stays home and has the babies (soul-winning on earth). And Christ as the husband brings home the bacon (blessings from heaven to the obedient).

CHAPTER 8

They Forgot Me

" . . . I was in prison and you came to visit me"

Matthew 25:36

The average believer desires to see everybody saved. But the Christian statistics show that 93% of all believers in North America forgot about the adults and children that are locked up. The majority of adult prisoners don't have a chance of receiving visitors or letters.

The origin of the institution

Define prison: a place of confinement for those convicted of contravening the laws of the state; most countries claim to aim also at rehabilitation. A Christian group called the Quakers, in the 17th century, founded the U.S. prison institution. Its members were called Quakers because their leader, George Fox, had once warned a Judge to "tremble and quake at the word of the Lord.

The original purpose

The original purpose was to make the prisoners disciples of Jesus Christ through evangelizing the institution. They also wanted to rehabilitate the prisoners, through counseling, prayer, and special training. To get them ready for the outside world. What did Jesus Christ say about this subject? He was in prison, and someone visited him. I need clothes and you clothed me, I was sick and you looked after me, I was in prison and you came to visit me. Matthew 25:36

Visit means a second chance, love in action and obedience to Jesus Christ. Whatever you did for the least you did for me. The king will reply, I tell you the truth, whatever you did for one of the least of these brothers of mine, you did for me. Matthew 25:40

How to set up a prison ministry

- Prepare a strong team within for prison ministry
- Prepare a radical method to present the word of God
- Prepare literature to hand out such as Bibles, tracts, newsletters, etc.
- Have a strong follow-up team for prisoners and families.
- Have letters, videos, and CD's ready to send to the chaplain

- Locate which institution you want to minister (youth home, prison, shelter, nursing home, etc.)
- Call the chaplain and get permission to come.
- Let him know how many people are on your team.
- What your agenda for ministry is.

Just because someone gets off track in life does not mean we should neglect him or her. The real truth about the matter is we all should have been locked up for the crimes we have committed against family, friends, co-workers, strangers and especially God. The only difference between the prisoners and us is that the authorities didn't catch us.

"You have heard that it was said to the people long ago, "Do not murder, and anyone who murders will be subject to judgment." But I tell you that anyone who is angry with his brother will be subject to judgment. Again, anyone who says to his brother, "Racca," is answerable to the Sanhedrin. But anyone who says, "you fool!" will be in danger of the fire of hell." Matthew 5:21,22

CHAPTER 9

Small Group Church

"Every day they continued to meet together in the temple courts. They broke bread in their homes and ate together with glad and sincere hearts, praising God and enjoying the favor of all the people. And the Lord added to their number daily those who were being saved."

Acts 2:46-47

Advantages of having a small group church

- It will close the back door of the church
- It will put fire back into evangelism
- Small groups offer a pastoral care structure second to none
- The church will grow in quality and quantity

The two weekly events

Weekly small groups

Sunday celebration

What is homogeneous? It is the same kind of people/group.

All of the small groups meet regularly for the purpose of spiritual edification and evangelistic outreach, with the goal of multiplication. All small groups are committed to participating in the functions of the local church weekly celebration and administration. Small groups multiply again and again because the same genetic make-up or quality control is transferred from group to group.

Make-up of small group

- Fellowship (eating food).
- Ice breaker (welcoming question).
- Worship & prayer (this draws the members into the presence of God).
- The word (cell lesson).
- Witness (requires the group to work together to win a lost soul/world for Christ Jesus).
- Group leaders must have a sign-in sheet with phone # of those in attendance.
- Group leaders must contact a visitor within 24 hours of the group lesson.
- Group leaders must encourage everybody to come to Sunday celebration service.
- Group leaders must always reveal the church's vision.
- Group ministry provides pastoral care, evangelism, counseling, follow-up, aftercare, discipleship, and all other important activities. The core organizational structure is based on group body ministry.

The church is of many members but one body. Just as the natural body must grow healthy, likewise the spiritual body. Therefore a group church must keep in mind that healthy growth is multiplying the way Christ want it. Jesus chose twelve men of different backgrounds, and out of those twelve he picked out three to impact greater things.

Having a small group does not mean that your church is a cell church. Many churches have cells, but the cells are not developing into other cells. Coming together to fellowship and singing does not institute a small group. There are such things called unhealthy cells in your body. When it becomes unhealthy, it starts the dying process. Therefore a cell group that is not part of a cell church will die.

What is a small group church?

"Day after day, in the temple courts and from house to house, they never stopped teaching and proclaiming the good news that Jesus is the Christ." Acts 5:42 In the book of Acts, we read that the early church went from house to house preaching Jesus. Notice that I said the church went from house to house. The cell church is a movement of God's people, always reaching out always intent on drawing in the unsaved, always concerned about the equipping of every single member to function under Christ's Lordship.

Small groups usually grow to 12 or 15 in 3 to 5 months. They then multiply into two groups. Saints who have the gift of teaching are discovered. This is how you make more disciples of Jesus Christ. In small groups, many needs are met for the edification of the church. For example, my church was in need of praise singers. During a small group fellowship, I discovered while in worship a couple of people who attended the small group had a heart to worship and could sing beautifully. After the fellowship, I went to them to see if we could meet on another day about being a part of our praise team.

A small group church is a church that recognizes there is a great harvest in the world. Nothing can stop a small group church from growing because it is very healthy. My prayer is that you begin to get busy in the field that is ready to be harvested. Do not stop working for the King of the Kingdom, for he is worthy to work for.

Small group lesson

The small group lesson is not designed to be a Bible study. Nor is it substituting or replacing mid-week church Bible study. The lesson is structured to get group participation with the purpose of ministering directly to individuals. Everyone will have a cell lesson in his or her hand, ready to read and give a word concerning the lesson.

The lesson should come from the senior pastor's Sunday morning message or from the pastor, which he has put together for the purpose of the small group. When we started our first small group years ago, I would write out the lesson dealing with issues of today. The Lord would give me deep subjects to talk about, and then I would build my lesson on that subject. This is an example of how God gave me a title for the small group, then I built a lesson on it. The lesson went like this:

Can't do it with two

"No one can serve two masters. Either he will hate the one and love the other, or he will be devoted to the one and despise the other. You cannot serve both God and money." Matthew 6:24

This is a very popular passage of scripture in the church, and even the unchurch is familiar with this verse in the Bible. People even make jokes about this scripture; they say, "baby you can't have two, because the good book said, no man can't serve two masters," in this week lesson we are going to deal with issues that relates to your allegiance to God or to another.

The message here is that Jesus wanted to know whom do they want to do it with. The question is doing what with? Jesus dealt with treasures, loyalty, how are you spending your time, and who are you spending your time with? Jesus said, "Do not store up for yourselves treasures on earth, where moth and rust destroy, and where thieves break in and steal. But store up for yourselves treasures in heaven, where thieves do not break in and steal. For where your treasure is, there your heart will be also." Matthew 6:19-21

What is Treasure?

Treasure is whatever is the most precious to you: objects, people, food, money, etc. It is what causes someone to spend all his or her energy and time protecting and adorning. Every woman, if they were truthfully earnest about jewelry, shopping, and even talking on the telephone. They would tell you that they really treasure these things.

Treasuring something can overtake you like nothing else can (good or bad). For example, sister Hot Dog used to dance all night long as a stripper, but one day she was invited to go to church with her brother, and after hearing the word of God she accepted Jesus as her personal Savior. And now she has a new lover and friend, Jesus Christ. She didn't stop dancing, but traded partners and now dances on a different floor. And now she's on the dance team at her church. Every time the church door opens, she's there ready to dance for Jesus Christ all night.

Statement: we need to find out what is overtaking us because it could easily be the wrong thing. It may be your charge card, food, sex, drugs, your job, and even that man you got. Jesus wants us to treasure him and his kingdom because you can't do it with two.

Nugget thought: treasure is always the object in the heart and thought of a person. Make sure that the right thing enters your heart and thought, because whatever is in you will always overtake you.

What is Heart?

Scriptural speaking, heart is from the word kardia, which means the seat of the desires, feeling, affection and passion for Godly and righteous things. Anything will attack our heart. The old proverbs said: “Above all else, guard your heart, for it affects everything you do.” Proverbs 4:23

The moment we stop guarding our hearts is the time the devil will have us for breakfast, lunch, and dinner. But guarding takes lots of work on the part of the believer. To guard is to protect, keep, to obey, and to observe. To not guard is to not obey, which in turn will allow your flesh to have its way. Once your flesh gets out of control, it will do with three and four at a time.

Statement: your heart should always be where Jesus is. When it is like that no matter what the devil tries to bring to the door of your heart you will not allow it to come in.

Nugget thought: the devil’s aims/purpose in the life of the believer is to make him/her have divided devotion. He knows that in a matter of time the believer will have a spiritual heart attack. Do not let this happen to you.

What is Thought?

Thought is the inner camera in one's life. Our thought is designed by God to take pictures of godly things, and frame it on our thought walls. Therefore, "focus" is the key in having a clear and holy picture. Have you ever heard, "What you see is what you get?" Well, here is another saying, "What you ponder, will cause one to wander."

It is very important that my thoughts are totally on the best object in the world, Jesus Christ. Let me put it like this, Jesus said: . . . ." love the Lord your God with all your heart and with all your soul and with all your mind." Matthew 22:37

This is a command and not a suggestion. For God does not want us to share our thoughts with drugs, illegal sex, anger, religion, etc.

Statement: do not allow your thought pattern get you in a position where your focus is on booty, the third leg, spiritual masturbation, which is a substitution for the real thing.

Nugget thought: the battleground is in your thought life. Your outer appearance may have a smile on it, but the inner man could be in battle. When you try to do it with two, you can bet your bottom dollar that you will lose the battle in your thought life.

Many people would come to the small group and leave touched, excited, and set free because of the many radical subjects we dealt with. Some were emotionally healed, became small group leaders, restored marriages, and great soul winners. Once again, I must say that the small group lesson is to minister and make disciples of Jesus Christ.

Remember, it's not a Bible class, nor is it a Sunday morning worship service. It is got to be on the personal side, or else it will become a Bible study or just another fellowship. And as you know, we have a lot of social fellowship going on in our churches.

CHAPTER 10

Pray for What

"The harvest is plentiful but the workers are few. Ask the Lord of the harvest, therefore, to send out workers into his harvest field." Matthew 9:37-38

Then he said to his disciples, "The harvest is plentiful but the workers are few. Ask the Lord of the harvest, therefore, to send out workers into the harvest field." Matthew 9:37,38

These words came directly from the mouth of Jesus in the book of Matthew. Jesus was going about in the towns, villages and in the synagogues preaching and teaching the good news of the kingdom. The signs and wonders that followed his message brought a great release on the people.

The religious leaders of that day had put such a heavy burden on the common people. Many could not keep up with the standard of the Pharisees who were the spiritual policemen and enemy of Christ. They had the look of righteousness but in reality their heart was wicked. They pretended to be for the common people but they were only thinking of their reputation and position.

It seems to be a transfer of attitudes and spirits from the Pharisees to the spiritual leaders of our day. We put heavy burdens on innocent people who truly love God. We come up with our own rules and traditions that make people fall through the cracks. And we are so concern about our title, position, and reputation, which makes us look so selfish.

Neither of these things matter when it comes down to the real reason for salvation.

"Jesus entered the temple area and drove out all who were buying and selling there. He overturned the tables of the money changers and the benches of those selling doves," it is written; he said to them, my house will be called a house of prayer, but you are making it a den of robbers." Matthew 21: 12-13

Jesus said this many years ago, and we are still dealing with the same things in our churches. Notice that he went into the temple area and not the political or the place where they partied. It was the place where the people came to worship God and to hear a word from the Lord.

Drove Out

Jesus Christ was angry because something had crept into the house of God. The purpose of the temple was fading away in the hearts of the people. "For the lips of a priest ought to preserve knowledge, and from his mouth men should seek instruction, because he is the messenger of the Lord almighty.

But you have turned from the way and by your teaching have violated the covenant with Levi, says the Lord almighty. So I have caused you to be despised and humiliated before all the people, because you have not followed my ways but have showed partiality in matters of the law." Malachi 2:7-9

Also, the godly reputation of the temple had changed from a place of prayer to a place of commercialism, merchandising and thieves. It truly vexed Jesus when he went to pray and found the people (leaders) playing in the temple area. He became a wild man and did not care about titles and started to wreck the place to put things back in order.

There must be a "driving" in the church so that we can put back in what belong. Now stop and think for a moment about the reputation of the church. Does it really stand for prayer, a seeking after God, and his divine will? Let me answer it No! The church has a new reputation and it is called commercialism, conferences, concerts, social parties, and merchandising. Notice that Jesus drove out the merchants and their customers first.

The Merchants

Church leaders have become merchants and not prayer leaders. We are selling man-made traditions to the people of God with no desire to repent. So the Pharisees and teachers of the law asked Jesus, "Why don't your disciples live according to the tradition of the elders instead of eating their food with unclean hands?" He replied, "Isaiah was right when he prophesied about you hypocrites; as it is written: 'These people honor me with their lips, but their hearts are far from me. They worship me in vain; their teachings are merely human rules (rules taught by men)." You have let go of the commands of God and are holding on to human traditions (the traditions of men)." And he continued, "You have a fine way of setting aside the commands of God in order to observe your own traditions." Mark 7:5-9

Jesus told the spiritual leaders of his day that you have let go of the commands of God and are holding on to the traditions of men. This sounds much like what goes on today. Our spiritual merchants have contaminated everything that God has place in the body of Christ for spiritual growth and edification.

For example, I was invited to a national day of prayer meeting where pastors and their congregation from all over came together to pray. I was so excited that people of different background, race, color, and denomination were coming together to seek God. I was truly expecting an atmosphere of seeking God when I walked in that place. But it was not so. One of the first things that grieved my spirit was that I had to pay ten dollars to get in, which will allow me to eat some fruit. Secondly, it felt like a social gathering. People were sitting around talking and exchanging business cards, drinking coffee, and looking cute. They also had a mini-concert by a recording artist at the prayer meeting. He sang, and they looked to him for entertainment.

The prayer meeting was commercialized and merchandized. It was well dressed up with a hint of making you fill very passive about the subject of prayer. America is in great trouble, and we were sitting there eating watermelon. The unborn in America are killed every ten minutes, and we were passing out business cards. There are more Christian marriages ending up in the divorce court then the non-Christians. You don't have to dress up prayer, just come together and pray. What do you think would have happened if four or five hundred people were on their faces before God without worrying about their clothes, title, and reputation? I believe a mighty outpouring of God would have taken place.

Merchant

The word merchant *means* the seller of goods. In Jesus' day, the merchants were the religious people who sold goods at a place that was supposed to represent something great. But it did not.

The Customers

Jesus drove out the buyers who came not to pray but play. The buyers of that day were the religious Jews who had a clear understanding of what the temple stood for. But they were so off focused that they could only see man-made stuff, stuff that had nothing to do with prayer but had everything to do with greed, folly, wastefulness, and idolatry.

Our modern day customers in the church are professional buyers who know exactly what they want. First of all, they have been in the church a long time and know how to budget for what they want. Many of them are pastors, evangelist, local church leaders, and old lay members. These buyers will consume up everything that has nothing to do with seeking after God.

Jesus was so fired up over these customers because all they do is buy-buy-buy. So Jesus showed them the door and said bye-bye-bye. I am sure the people of that day had a problem with the way Jesus handle those wasteful consumers. But Jesus did not care because he had a zeal that could not be put out.

We as saints of the Most High God must be like Jesus in a way that we will not put up with people who come into the church and consume up stuff. When will we get sick and tired of all the mess that goes on in the church, when will we stop playing church, when will we get back to praying in the church? Come on let's drive out foolishness. We may lose our friends that led us to be consumers. We may lose our titles that man gave us. It may even mess up our little reputations that we have tried to hold on to. Come on, let's drive it out!

The Harvest is Plenty

Jesus got into Peter's boat and asked him to put out a little from the shore. Then Jesus began to teach the people from the boat. After Jesus had finished speaking, he told Peter to put it out into deep water and let down the nets for a catch. Jesus was about to demonstrate what he was teaching so that it will become a reality to the hearers.

Peter was a little hesitant because they had fish and worked all night long and had not caught anything. But Peter said because you said so, I will let down the nets. When Peter begin to submit to the will of God, then God showed up in a greater way. They caught such a large number of fish that their nets began to break. At that point, they needed more help and, their partners came and filled the boats so full that they began to sink.

How do we know that the harvest is plentiful? Well, the answer is right in the miracle of catching a large sum of fish. Jesus knew beforehand that the catch would be so great just to get their attention. Christ has shown the church over and over again that there is a harvest that is ready and ripe for his people to go get them. A matter a fact, Christ had already prepared the field for the church. For the Bible said that the field is his anyway. So that means there are places where people are waiting to be brought into the kingdom of God. But it won't happen until we as His workmanship/servants start to get busy right now.

I remember some years ago that I had the opportunity to go out alone with a few people from a church of four hundred members. We went out into the neighborhood sharing the good news of Christ. We noticed that a lady sitting on her porch enjoying the wonderful weather and reading her Saturday newspaper. So we walked toward the lady's house and got her attention and started to talk with her. I told her who I was and that I was from the church on the corner. Then I said that God had a gift for you, and she cut me off while I was talking and said that she has been living in this house for fifteen years, and no one has never come over to her house to share any good news (the gospel) with her. When she said that, I realized that she was ready to receive Christ. At that moment, we took advantage of the moving of the Holy Spirit, and she received Jesus as her Savior.

Another thing about the harvest is that it is the pathway to many of our blessings. "I tell you the truth," Jesus replied, "no one who has left home or brothers or sisters or mother or father or children or fields for me and the gospel will fail to receive a hundred times as much in this present age (homes, brother, sisters, mothers, children and fields and with them, persecutions) and in the age to come, eternal life." Mark 10:29-30

Jesus was saying a couple of things here in these verses that we overlook. First of all, he was saying that we must prioritize our life for him and the gospel. It must be first things first. Jesus made it known to his disciples that he must be first in their life. If God so loved the world that he gave, we too must give back to him our entire life. But the problem that we face right now is that there is a great service that is going on, and it is called "lip service." Jesus told the leaders of his day: "These people honor me with their lips, but your hearts are far from me. They worship me in vain; their teachings are but rules taught by men." Matthew 15:8

Do not get mad at the red-letter edition in your bible, Jesus was talking to the church folks. Many of us say that we love him but do not obey him. And I am not talking about going to church and singing in the choir or getting your goosebumps on in Sunday morning worship. But I am talking about having an ongoing relationship with him, which lead you to live a life of obedience to him.

Putting Christ first is not praying first thing in the morning and then not having a self-controlled life throughout the day. Most of us say he is first because we sought the Lord this morning. But the problem with that is our co-worker does not see Christ in us, the one we pray to every morning. Our husbands cannot stand our attitudes, so he leaves the house for a while until you go to sleep. Christ truly wants to be first by you, showing forth his glory right here on earth.

Would you believe that Christ said that he wants us to prioritize our life so that the gospel be first in a way that you are living the good news right now? In other words, you become the good news. After becoming the good news, then you are compelled to take (yourself) the good news to those who are living in bad news. We are to take the good news to those dark places, which many of us are too scared to go because the gospel is not first in our life.

When the gospel is first it is all you think about. There is nothing in this entire world that cannot stop you from putting the gospel first. You will find ways to improve your strategy in presenting the gospel. You will search down places where people are hurting, and I am not talking about the people that are in the church hurting, because someone hurt their feelings. But I am talking about going outside of the four walls of your church.

Do not be afraid

In this story Jesus left with a powerful statement, "don't be afraid; from now on, you will catch men." Fear overcame Peter in a way that he wanted to run away from the will of Christ. For Peter had never seen anything like that. Fear is the enemy of the will of God, which always attacks your righteous actions. It will make you go the opposite way, which is out of the will of God.

Jesus was using something in the natural realm to show the people something by using the natural. The natural went to another level because of the divine message. That is just like Jesus, because everything he touches goes to another level, whether it is natural or Spiritual. But fear will always stop the move of God no matter what he is manifesting in your life. Like Peter, you too will hear the voice of Christ say to you "do not be afraid."

I mentioned earlier that I went to Philadelphia, Pennsylvania, to preach in an area that was very dangerous. I remembered, after arriving there the first night while sleeping, I awoke in the middle of the night. Then I saw what appeared to be a huge man in the dark looking over me. My first thought was to get up and run out of the room and never return. However, I said to myself, "Lord, please get me out of here and return me back to Detroit where my family is." I, in other words, I cried out, "Momma help me, help me, I want to go home!"

After realizing that something or someone was in my room, I put the blanket over my head just like a little kid would do. Then the Spirit of the Lord told me to take my head from under that blanket and look at the image. My mind wanted to tell God are you crazy, do you really know what I want to do? Well, just like Peter, I took God at his word and took the blanket from off my head and looked at the huge scary image right in his face.

When I looked at him, my mouth began to open and my lips started to move. I was amazed at what I heard come out of my mouth, but I said it anyway. I told that image I was not scared, and I knew who he was and where he came from. Then I said in the name of Jesus, "I command you to leave this room right now so I can sleep and preach Jesus in the morning. Also, you evil spirit, I am not going anywhere until God is finished with me in this city, so goodbye, and then I fell asleep. The next morning the team and I went witnessing, and we led people from off the street to Jesus. Then I preached in the evening service and witnessed so many people give their life to Christ.

You see, I realized that it was the spirit of fear that was in my room. And it was trying to get me to run off from the mandate that God gave me for Philadelphia. But once you overcome fear, then that is the time you will see a greater manifestation of God in your life. Your personal life, marriage, business, and ministry will go to another level. You will enter into another dimension of power.

Catch

"Then Jesus said to Simon, "don't be afraid; from now on you will catch men."

Breaking the nets and sinking a boat with fish was a picture of the harvest that was to come through the obedience of the disciples. Instead of catching White Bass, they will catch white men. Instead of catching Red Pickerel, they will catch red men. Instead of catching Black Bass, they will catch black men. Jesus was letting them know that there was going to be a new type of fish that they were to catch.

This word *catch* is a unique word in the Greek. Luke 5:10 is the only place where you will find it in the entire Bible. And it is one of the most powerful words that Jesus has ever spoken. The Greek word is Zogreo, and it means to "catch men alive" in other words, you catch fish and then it dies, but now you will catch something else, and it will live forever . . . soul of men.

What Jesus told his disciples two thousand years ago, goes for us right now in the 21st century. He told his disciples do not fear. He is talking to you brother John, Chris, Harry, Jimbo, Chris Brown and the list goes on. He told his disciples catch souls alive. He's talking to you sister Lisa, Mary, Alice, Mattie Pearl, and Lady Gaga. He told his disciples to pray for workers. He's talking to you Evangelist, Aretha. He told his disciples to make disciples. He is talking to you Pastor, Donald. His words are old and ancient, but relevant.

Radical Evangelism

We have a lot to talk about concerning radical evangelism. First of all, there are a lot of believers, church members, tongue talkers and bible tokers out there sitting doing nothing with the gift that God has given them. I recognize these people as having an S.U. degree "saved and useless." Too many believers know all the scriptures about soul winning and how Jesus cast out demons. But just knowing the scriptures isn't going to save one soul from hell.

It is time for us as saints of the Most High God to take our rightful place right here on earth. I am sick and tired of seeing believers go to church thinking that they can defeat the devil with all of the jumping and shouting. Some of us can't even get along with each other in the church. The devil got us fighting each other, which brings about a division in the church.

Our objective in this warfare is to kick the devil's natural butt. However, the only way we're going to beat him down is when we as believers decide to be united as one body. "My prayer is not for them alone, I pray also for those who will believe through their message, that all of them may be one, Father, just as you are in me and I am in you. May they also be in us so that the world may believe that you have sent me. I have given them the glory that you gave me, that they may be one as we are one: I in them and you in me. May they be brought to complete unity to let the world know that you sent me and have loved them even as you have loved me." Jesus said, "the gates of hell will not prevail against the church." I truly believe what Jesus said in the word of God. But I want to give you something to think about which will convince you to do something.

I live in a state, which is broking down in counties, and in these many different counties, there are dozens of local churches. I presently live in Wayne, County, where there are more than 4000 churches. And many of them are literally next to each other with some sharing of the same church building. I am not saying something is wrong or right with that. But the smaller church is trying to stay alive with just a handful of members while the larger church flourish by welcoming members from the smaller church.

Studies show that where there are more churches in a neighborhood, crime is higher. Not only is crime higher, but also fewer souls are being saved. Do not forget what Jesus said: "And I tell you that you are Peter, and on this rock I will build my church, and the gates of Hades will not overcome it." Matthew 16:18

I believe something is wrong with this picture For Jesus never lied to anybody, nor can he lie at all. Therefore, it is the church that is making him out to be a liar. It is time to stand at the gate and battle by using the principles of radical evangelism. Now I'll explain the difference between evangelism and radical evangelism. First of all, let me make it known that it is sad that I have to make a distinction between the two. Evangelism should be just what it is.

A few years ago, I went to an evangelism training seminar, hoping to better my skills in winning souls for Christ. So I went to the seminar with an opened mind to receive what God had for me. But what I saw and learned truly disappointed me and even grieved my spirit. There were people at the seminar who didn't even know how to give their testimony on how they got saved. Many didn't have a clear understanding about the gospel of Jesus Christ themselves. The sad part about this is the instructors were telling us to pass out gospel tracts and then promote your local church. Now is that evangelism? No!

The church that I pastored went out into the neighborhood to win souls for Christ one Saturday morning. As we approached the resident's door, I knocked with excitement. I knew there was a clear word of God in my spirit for this person. An elderly lady came to the door with fear in her eyes, and said, "Who is it?" I said with compassion but yet with boldness in my voice, "Robert Shackleford. The Lord sent me here to tell you that you need a healing in your body, and he's going to heal you right now." Then she opened the door and we began to pray for her, and God healed her. Now that is an example of radical evangelism.

There was another time when our church went to a public school to preach the gospel of Jesus Christ. I brought with me our D.R.A.M.A. (delivering real answers with music and acting) team. The principal of that school closed down the entire school so that we could minister to the students as well as the teachers. After we finished singing, rapping, and acting I began to preach the raw word of God. While preaching I began to take notice of the crowd. Many of the kids were weeping, some were embracing each other, and some rushed out of the auditorium, not wanting anybody to see them cry. After preaching, I called an altar call right there in the public school here in America.

My ministers and I began to pray for the students and teachers that responded to the word of God. When we were at the altar, and even afterwards, the students began to share their hurts and pain with us. Some were hurt because their father molested them. Some were hurt because their mothers were out on the street selling their bodies. And many of the boys were carrying anger, rage, and hatred in them toward someone else. But God saved and healed a multitude of people that day. Now that is radical evangelism!

Now the first step to radical evangelism is for the believer to know Jesus. I am not talking about Him as your Savior, friend, and way maker; of course that's first things first. I am talking about as an evangelist, preacher, and prophet.

When you know him as an evangelistic preacher and prophet, then you will try to imitate him. The only way to know and imitate Jesus is through much prayer and studying the word of God. Also, you need to get hooked up in a church that does radical evangelism on a regular basis so you can put into practice what you were taught.

The second step is to have a strategy on how you are going to win souls for Christ. Anybody can walk the streets and say God loves you. But in some cases, it is going to take more than that. We, as a people must learn how to plan out our work for Christ. Sometimes it may take days or even weeks before you go forth with your plan. Having a plan is the beginning of the battle.

Something very evil happened to us here in America on September 11, 2001. Personally, I believe it took much time to plan that wicked event. Satan is a great strategist, who has nothing but time on his hand. As I just stated, this evil event took place on 9/11. Let us look at some facts:

1. September 11th is the 254th day of the year, 2+5+4=11.
2. After September 11th, there are 111 days left to the end of the year.

3. The twin towers standing side by side looked like the number 11.
4. The state of New York was the 11th state added to the union.
5. And New York City has 11 letters in it.

Some of this may be coincidence or part of the evil plan, I do not know. My point is that if Satan is a strategist, then we must be better than he is in going into his camp. The third step is very simple; as I stated earlier in this book . . . just go!

Go is very important in the life of the believer. Go, in the eyes of Jesus, is always going out. Jesus said, “go ye therefore.” The church said, “stay ye, therefore.” All hell breaks out when you stand still not doing kingdom work. What I am trying to convey is that the reason why we struggle so much in our lives is because we are not busy in the things of God.

An Answered Prayer

I cannot understand the mind of Christ when he say things sometimes, for example: "Then he said to his disciples, the harvest is plentiful but workers are few. Ask the Lord of the harvest, therefore, to send out workers into his harvest fields." Matthew 9:37-38 Jesus told his disciples to pray to the Lord of the harvest, that he will send out workers into his harvest field. Then he turned around and sent the same people that he told to pray concerning the harvest out into the harvest field.

These twelve Jesus sent out with the following instructions; "Do not go among the Gentiles or enter any town of the Samaritans. Go rather to the lost sheep of Israel. As you go, preach this message: The Kingdom of heaven is near." Matthew 10:5-7 I may not clearly understand word for word what Jesus says at times but you can be for sure that I can follow his examples and commands.

His command to his disciples is telling me that the prayer for workers to be sent out has been answered. In other words, there is no real need for me to spin hours in prayer for God to send more help out into his field. Instead, I need to get busy doing what Jesus wants me to do. Go Get Them! Then

God will supply what is needed in my level of ministry. And if all believers would do the same, then we can win this world without a shadow of a doubt.

I am not saying that we should stop praying for help to complete the will of God. However, we do need to start letting our nets down now because the blessing is in your obedience to God's word. We on the other hand, make so many excuses for not catching souls alive. Some people leave it up to their church evangelism department. And some leave it up to a TV evangelist by sending money to that ministry. Christ did not say leave it up to somebody else. He left it up to you to do the job, and he is counting on you to accomplish it.

Every year our church hosts a conference called "Zogreo." It is an evangelism conference, which trains and prepares God's people for the harvest. I remember our first meeting in October of 1996. I had received so many calls from pastors, friends, and people who wanted to attend. There were many promises from so many people who said that they were coming. We spent so much money on advertisement for the conference. But sad to said that not even one hundred people attended the conference. Some nights there were thirty people and that was the largest attendance. It wasn't that we didn't have great speakers, for we had well known and anointed speakers and recording artist.

My point in telling you this is because people are not interested in being equipped for working in God's harvest field. If we had a prophetic conference, then there would not have been a problem in packing the house out each night. No matter who's speaking at the meeting, it would have been standing room only.

Sacrifice

Our heavenly father is a God of sacrifices. What I mean is that he is the great giver to all men. He gave the greatest sacrifice to us that we might have everlasting life. Not only should we have eternal life but that we may live on earth with total peace and joy full of the Holy Spirit. Now we all, you that know God dwells in us right now. And since he does live in us, we must be like him in the area of sacrifice. We were designed to sacrifice unto God for the benefit of showing forth his glory here on earth. Our blessing comes when we sacrifice to God on a daily basis.

What is Sacrifice?

- Old Testament way – it is killing something
- It is given something to
- It is worship to God
- It is praises to God
- Works of charity to men
- Spiritual service unto God

In the Hebrew and Greek language, one word could mean many things. That is why it is important when you are studying God's word and go back to the original language to find out what was really said. The Hebrew meaning for sacrifice is to slaughter, offering, and victim.

The Greek meaning for sacrifice is to make an offering. In the New Testament, we are the sacrifice of God, not in a sense of literally killing ourselves, but killing our flesh. Fulfilling Christ's command concerning the harvest all by itself is a sacrifice. Your flesh does not want to go beyond the four walls and Go Get Them. But in order to receive an outpouring of God, you must kill the flesh daily.

Just then, his disciples returned and were surprised to find him talking with a woman. But no one asked, "what do you want?" or "why are you talking with her?" John 4:27 Our Savior Jesus Christ was the greatest example in reaching the unreachable. He would eat, talk, sleep, and walk with the insignificant. The gospel of John tells the story of how Jesus ministered to a woman and not only a woman, but also a woman who was a Samaritan. He laid the foundation in going into places that were not popular. Jesus said to pray, and then he sent them out to fulfill that request. He did not say go to the rich only or to one particular color. He said, "Go Get Them!"

There are places that we fail to go to do the work of the Lord. There are people that we do not want to deal with because they do not look or talk like us. For example, many of us feel so intimidated when a Jehovah's Witness confronts us. Not knowing that we should confront them without any fear in us.

The Jehovah's Witness needs eternal life also. So why would we overlook them and others? Jesus said fear no man, but only him who can cast you into the lake of fire. So therefore, let us witness to those who are blind to the truth of Christ.

Jehovah's Witness – Charles Taze Russell (1852 - 1916) founded the organization, and later Joseph F. Rutherford. It began in 1879 in Pennsylvania, and now its headquarters are in Brooklyn, New York. The new world translation is what they say is the Holy Bible. The leaders of the organization translated it. They also have all current watchtower publication, which includes the reasoning from the scriptures, you can live forever in paradise on earth, watchtower and awake magazines.

What They Believe:

God: One – person God, called Jehovah. No trinity. Jesus is the first thing Jehovah created.

Jesus: Jesus is not God. Before he lived on earth, he was Michael, the archangel. Jehovah made the universe through him, and on earth he was a man who lived a perfect life. After dying on a stake (not a cross), he was resurrected as a spirit; his body was destroyed. Jesus is not coming again; he "returned" invisibly in 1914 in spirit. Very soon, he and the angels will destroy all non-Jehovah's Witnesses. Holy Spirit: impersonal "holy spirit" is not God, but rather an invisible, active force from Jehovah.

Salvation: be baptized as Jehovah's Witnesses. Most followers must earn everlasting life on earth by "door-to-door work." Salvation in heaven is limited to 144,000 "anointed ones." This number is already reached.

Other beliefs: known as the Watchtower Bible and Tract Society. Meet on Sundays in kingdom halls. Active members encouraged to distribute literature door-to-door. Once a year, the Lord's evening meal; only "anointed" ones may partake. Do not vote, salute the flag, work in the military, or accept blood transfusions.

Mormonism (latter-day saints), a young man by the name of Joseph Smith, Jr. (1805 – 1844), founded the Church of Jesus Christ of the Latter-Day Saints in 1830, in New York. The headquarters is now in Salt Lake, Utah.

The book of Mormon, doctrine and covenants, the pearl of great price, and smith's inspired version are the writings they read and live by.

What they believe:

God: God the father was once a man, but became God

and has a physical body, as does his wife (heavenly mother). No trinity. Father, Son, and Holy Spirit are three separate gods themselves.

Jesus: Jesus is a separate God from the father (Elohim). He was created as a spirit child by the father and mother in heaven and is the elder brother of all men and spirit beings. His body was created through a sexual union between Elohim and Mary. Jesus was married. His death on the cross does not provide full atonement for all sins but does provide everyone with resurrection.

Holy Spirit: is a God separate from the father and the Son. Holy Spirit is a fluid-like substance by which the father exercises his influence.

Salvation: resurrected by grace but saved (exalted to Godhood) by works, including faithfulness to church leaders, Mormon baptism, tithing, ordination, marriage, and secret temple rituals. There is no eternal life without Mormon membership.

Other beliefs: no alcohol, tobacco, coffee, or tea. Baptism on behalf of the dead and two year missionary commitment is encouraged, door to door proselytizing. Secret temple rituals available only to members in good standing. People of African ancestry not granted full access to Mormon priesthood and privileges until 1978.

Islam: Muhammad was the leader of the Islamic faith in A.D. 610 in Mecca and Medina. Headquarters in Mecca, Saudi Arabia, main sects, sunni and sh'ite.

Writings: Koran, scripture in Arabic. Hadith (Muhammad's words and deeds). Biblical law of moses, Psalms, and the gospel of Jesus (the Injil accepted by Koran, but considered by Muslims to be "corrupted").

God: God (Allah) is one. God revealed the Koran to Muhammad through the angel Gabriel. God is a severe Judge (though sometimes merciful) and is not depicted as loving.

Jesus: Jesus is one of up to 124,000 prophets sent by God to various cultures. Abraham, Moses, and Muhammad are others. Jesus was born of a virgin but is not the son of God. Sinless, not divine or God himself. He was not crucified (he ascended to heaven without dying). He is referred to as messiah and ayatollah (sign of God). Jesus will return in the future to live and die.

Holy Spirit: the Koran refers to Jesus as Spirit of God. Muslim scholars see the angel Gabriel as the Holy Spirit.

Salvation: humans are basically good, but fallible and need guidance. The balance between good and bad deeds determines eternal destiny in paradise or hell. God's mercy may tip the balances, but it is arbitrary and uncertain.

Other beliefs: followers are called Muslims. Go to the mosque for prayers, sermons, and counsel holy efforts to spread Islam (jihad). Five pillars of Islam: confess that Allah is the one true God and that Muhammad is his prophet. They pray five times daily facing Mecca. Give alms (money). Fast during the month of Ramadan, making pilgrimage to Mecca (once in a lifetime).

New Age: It is based on eastern mystics, Hinduism, and paganism. Popularized in part by actress, like Shirley Maclaine.

Key Writings: no holy book. Use selected Bible passages; Hindu, Buddhist, and Taoist writings; and Native American beliefs, writings on astrology, mysticism, and magic.

God: everything and everybody is God. God is an impersonal force or principle, not a person. People have unlimited inner power and need to discover it.

Jesus: Jesus is not the one true God. He is not a Savior, but a spiritual model, and guru, and is now an "ascended master." He was a new ager who tapped into divine power in the same way that anyone can. Many believe he went east to India or Tibet and learned mystical truths. He did not rise physically, but rose into a higher spiritual realm.

Holy Spirit: sometimes a psychic force. Man is divine and can experience psychic phenomena such as contacting unearthly beings.

Salvation: need to offset bad karma with good karma. Can tap into supernatural power through meditation, self-awareness, TM and spirit guides. Use terms such as reborn for this new self-awareness.

Other beliefs: Can include yoga, meditation, visualization, astrology, channeling, hypnosis, trances, tarot card readings, and contact with spirits. Use of crystals to get in harmony with God (energy), for psychic healing, for contact with spirits and for developing higher consciousness, or other psychic powers, strive for world unity and peace and holistic health.

Now you know that there is a need for the church to get up off their knees and get out into the harvest field of God. For there are a whole lot of people out there who are blind to the truth of God and do not know it. But we have the answers through the word of God. Know for sure that the harvest is ripe for the church to reap. No longer can you make excuses about yourself. You have the ability to change lives by the power of God. Therefore go back to your church and ask your pastor, "What are we really doing in our community?" And, "Will you train me to Go Get Them?"

CHAPTER 11

The Final Word

"Finally be strong in the Lord and in his mighty power."

Ephesians 6:10

But some of them became obstinate; they refused to believe and publicly maligned the Way. So Paul left them. He took the disciples with him and had discussions daily in the lecture hall of Tyrannus. This went on for two years, so that all the Jews and Greeks who lived in the province of Asia heard the word of the Lord (Acts 19:9,10).

These passages in the book of Acts are part of my favorite throughout the entire Bible. Because it tells of the great story of how one man proclaimed the word of God continually for two years. And, that Jews and Greeks from a large area heard the word.

What is wrong with us that we have a couple hundred or more churches in one zip code. With so many churches, we can win an entire city. It does not take a lot of people to work the harvest in your home, community, job, and city. But it does take a persistent believer like the apostle Paul/you.

My friend, the Apostle Paul, was in a hard place while ministering in the city of Ephesus. First, it started with people who had received John's baptism, but had not been baptized with the Holy Spirit, which would accompany their faith in the Lord.

Second, Paul saw the need to stay in that paganistic city, that many may know Christ. And after staying there, he was used by God to demonstrate His power to work extraordinary miracles, so that even handkerchiefs and aprons that had touched him were taken to the sick.

Third, there were some who tried to go out evangelize in the streets, but the spiritual gang members beat them down. Would you believe that it was preacher kids of that day who got whipped in the streets by the spiritual gang members? Yes, it is true!

Dear friends, please hear my heart when I say that there are people right in your surroundings who have never heard the gospel. You do not have to go and preach in a foreign country to preach Christ because there is truly a great harvest in your backyard.

I was sent to help plant a church in the inner city of Detroit some years ago. We were out in the neighborhood telling people about Jesus. I started sharing the gospel with two teenagers who lived in the neighborhood. I asked them, "Have you heard of Jesus Christ?" The answer that they gave me was breathtaking.

They said, “we have never heard of Jesus Christ ever before.” It truly shocked me to hear that right in this big city of Detroit, where there are thousands of churches. These two teenage girls did not know Jesus died on the cross for their sins.

It is important that you see the need to go out and be a witness for Christ. Jesus saw the crowd and had compassion on them. Therefore, he saw the need to do something about their hurt, pain, sickness, and spiritual blindness. We must do the same if we truly want to please Him. Once you began to fulfill the need, then you can be for sure that Christ will use you to demonstrate his love. Some will get saved with a desire to live for Christ whole-heartedly. Some will receive healing in their life. However, God does it, you can be confident that God will use you.

I was told by the Holy Spirit to start a church in a city where nobody knew me, and I didn’t know them. I had no resources in starting a church, and naturally speaking, all odds was against me. The Holy Spirit said go but I had no money, no connections, no building, no members, no musician, and no equipment. The city was 86% white and 4% black with more corn fields than ever. It was like going to a foreign country without having no money and no place to live. However, after reading in Ephesians 6:10, "Finally, be strong in the Lord and in his mighty power," I submitted to the Holy Spirit and started the process of planting a church in Monroe, Michigan. Every Saturday for weeks, I drove all by myself 40 miles doing door to door ministry and shared the gospel to every person who opened the door.

I always say, "obey God and leave the consequences to him." Things begin to come together because of my obedience to God. Just before our open day of the new church, I was invited to preach in another city. When the church service was ending, a major grocery store executive was there to hear me preach and came up to me and said that he has some equipment that he wanted to donate to our new church. Well, I wasn't sure what all he had to give, but after three days he pulled up in a truck and pulled out so much music equipment to start up a 1000 seat church. I thought that I was dreaming because I saw God give me more than enough. Now we need a building to hold our worship service and store all of this expensive equipment.

I continue to win souls for Christ each week, I did not

let anybody or the weather stop me from displaying the power of God on the porches, doorsteps, backyards, and on the sidewalks. There was a school in the area of where I was praying and winner souls for Christ. I called the school administration and asked if we can use the gym of the school for Sunday worship. I got a yes answer from the administration, it was that easy.

God was truly faithful to this new church. I saw in the first grand opening of our worship service people from the neighborhood walking to church. No one knew me, but they were introduced to Jesus weeks before on the streets. That first service set the stage for the supernatural to hit this new church. People received Christ, got emotionally and physically healed. Each week God was adding to our new church, we were putting out more chairs every Sunday. The favor of God was on us to be a blessing to the people who join this new church.

As the church begins to grow, we started to mobilize it for evangelism. We do not have an evangelism team or department; I teach that the entire church is the team. So every Sunday before worship, the church goes out into the neighborhood to share the gospel of Christ. Then we bring them to Sunday worship and watch God restore lives. I cannot imagine what would happen if I did not obey the Holy Spirit. The city Newspaper had our church in the News talking about what we were doing in this city. Drug transitional home opened up for us which allow us to display the power of Jesus Christ. I got to say it again, obey God and leave the consequences to him.

Every time the church goes out to share the gospel, we see a mighty demonstration of the power of God. I remember going to this one house and knocked on the door. I told the person who came to the door, "Jesus said he is going to heal your mother." The lady responded by saying, "I will let her know, she went to her doctor's appointment a few hours ago." We left and went to another house, but nobody was home. However, before I could reach the sidewalk, I heard a voice saying, "Pastor, I need to talk with you." So I turned and noticed that it was an older lady who came out of the house next door. It was the younger lady's mother that I told was healed. I turned and said to her, "Yes, I would love to talk with you. The lady told me with so much excitement that she went to the hospital because of cancer." However, the doctor told her that she does not have cancer in her body, and they do not understand why. She also said that her daughter told her you came to our door and told her that your mother is healed, and I want to ask how you knew that I had cancer. I told her the Holy Spirit told me and laid my hand on her immediately, and prayed for her right on the sidewalk. The lady fell to her knees and wept. She kept saying, “Thank you, Jesus.”

Go Get Them saints, for it is truly ripe, and do not listen to people when they say negative things like: it is dangerous out there, nobody will listen to you, and you not called to do this. You can do it and show forth the Power of the Holy Spirit wherever you go. Your blessings are in obeying Jesus Christ. “I tell you the truth,” Jesus replied, “no one who has left home or brothers or sisters or mother or father or children or fields for me and the gospel will fail to receive a hundred times as much in this present age (homes, brothers, sisters, mothers, children, and fields-and with them, persecutions) and in the age to come, eternal life. Mark 10:29-30

Brother Willis used to be a gang leader before he accepted Christ. He recruited so many young men to be on his team to do bad things. Brother Willis spent a lot of time in prison, and while he was in prison, Jesus saved him. When he got out of prison, nothing could stop him from telling people about Jesus. He would walk up and down the street in his old neighborhood, sharing his testimony. However, Brother Willis joined a church that did not go beyond the four walls of the church building. Brother Willis wanted to build a team for Jesus better than he did for Satan. The church wanted to build a team for the church and the pastor. So the people in the church told him that we do not want people who have ear and nose rings on their faces. They told him that we do not believe in tattoos, so do not bring people here who have them on their bodies. Brother Willis was so discourage about the support and response that he got from his church. He wanted to go get the harvest for Christ because of the love he had for him. He knew that the answer to his dying community was Jesus Christ. Eventually, Brother Willis left that church and joined another one (the one I pastored). He wanted to be around people who were on fire for Jesus and the gospel.

Saints, my desire is that after you read this book, you will be so encourage telling your story about Jesus Christ to as many people that you can. You may be the only John the Baptist in your home, on your job, or maybe in your church.

Whatever you do, never stop being a voice crying out to a hurting people.

ABOUT THE AUTHOR

At the age of 5, Bishop R.J. Shackleford recorded his first family record. People from all over would want to hear this little boy sing and dance all over the stage. He appeared on live television and radio as a little boy along with his father and brothers, singing songs of the Lord. A few years later at the age of 7, he preached his first sermon. Bishop R.J. Shackleford knew at an early age that he wanted to be a preacher and singer. Therefore at the age of 12, he accepted his call into the ministry. The ministry of Bishop R.J. Shackleford was in great demand as a young preacher. He would travel all across this country preaching the gospel of Jesus Christ. Later on, he was called to plant his first church, Fruit of The Spirit Family Outreach Church. While leading that great congregation, God began to use him to write songs for the nations. Bishop R.J. Shackleford has shared the stage with gospel giants such as the late Dr. Myles Monroe, Rance Allen, and Pastor Al Green just to name a few. Bishop R. J. Shackleford operates in the supernatural and radical evangelism. He has a blessing and healing ministry where people from all over the world has received instant supernatural miracles. He is the founding pastor of Zogreo Family Church in Monroe, Michigan, where he started by knocking on doors sharing the love of Jesus Christ.

The ministry of Bishop R.J. Shackleford is in great demand around this country. He can be heard and seen on international Radio/TV each week on The Worship Network (worshipcenterradio.net). His program "Miracles For Me Now" is heard in over 60 countries and growing. Bishop R.J. Shackleford is also the book author of *Eating My Way To Heaven*. He is training and raising up prayer warriors from all over the world through his weekly prayer service. The fire of the man of God seems to never go out.

www.ingramcontent.com/pod-product-compliance
Lightning Source LLC
LaVergne TN
LVHW010102110826
845155LV00028B/451